The DUCK
SHACK

Cover Illustration by Margarita Sikorskaia

Softcover ISBN 13: 978-1-7346743-4-7
Hardcover ISBN 13: 978-1-7346743-5-4

Printed in the United States of America

Cover and interior design by James Monroe Design, LLC.

Lucky Luke, LLC.
4335 Matthew Court
Eagan, Minnesota 55123

www.KevinLovegreen.com
Quantity discounts available!

Chapter 1

It's late. We're driving in the Suburban. Tomorrow is the opening day of duck season. I can't wait!

It's a long drive to the duck shack, though. I close my eyes and tuck my head into my soft pillow against the car door.

A vision of last year's duck opener is burned into my memory. Playing it like a movie in my mind, I relive one of the amazing moments from that early Saturday morning . . .

A huge flock of twenty giant mallards circled the bouncing decoys we had set out on the cold water. The ducks were almost close enough to shoot—but not quite. Dad held us back.

The leader of the flock steered the others out to the big water. But then she circled them back. She couldn't resist the decoys' invitation.

The flock headed right to us. I could see the green heads of the male ducks shimmering in the early morning sun. The flock was now following our string of decoys. We might as well have been reeling them right to our laps.

Closer they came. I could hear a couple of them quacking. We stayed perfectly still. We didn't want to flare them.

My eyes got bigger with each flap of their wings. My heart pounded. My hands gripped my trusty 20-gauge tight. My finger was on the safety, ready to free my gun for action.

They came right over our decoys. Half of them set their wings, committed to landing on the water.

Then I heard Dad's magic words: "Take 'em!"

I jumped up and locked on a giant green head right in front of me. I pulled my gun tight to my cheek and looked down the barrel. A racing drake turned hard to my right. As I followed him, the gun flowed as if it were a part of me.

At last, I pulled my bead on the barrel in front of him and let the shot fly. He *folded up, fell through the air, and crashed into the water.*

The feeling of victory overtook my body! My heart pounded even harder than before.

Duck hunting is awesome!

Suddenly, a bump in the road causes my head to slip from the pillow. It brings me back to reality. I take a deep breath and open my eyes.

The Suburban's headlights are bouncing off the endless trees as we splash through mud puddles and crawl over the uneven road. We left the safety of the blacktop two miles ago. We're almost to the shack!

I look over at my sister, Crystal. She had been dozing against the other door in the back seat, but now she's awake too.

She brushes her hair out of her eyes. She and I have the same color of hair—red. We got that from Dad. Crystal's hair is by far the longest, though. It goes below her shoulders.

I'm Luke. I love hunting and fishing more than you can imagine. My dad has been taking Crystal and me into the woods and out on the water since we were tiny.

Crystal is a year and a half older than me. She loves the outdoors too. Even though she loves hunting, she's not *quite* as crazy about it as Dad and I are. She also loves volleyball, which gets in the way of hunting at times. Thankfully, she could make it this weekend for the duck opener. It's cool having her around.

The final dirt road before the driveway into the duck shack is long and rough. It loves trying to suck your tires into the mud. We've made many trips up and down this road, and Dad's expert driving hasn't failed us yet. We always make it! This time is no different.

The old yard light fills the final stretch of the driveway, welcoming us. The little red cabin we call the duck shack is in sight. This place has turned into one of my favorite places to be.

Dad and three of his hunting buddies bought the duck shack years ago. It's tucked back in the woods, just off Leech Lake in northern Minnesota. Leech is a giant lake with a bunch of back channels and bays.

Our bay is shallow. Most of it is only five feet deep. The bottom is mucky and soft, which isn't great for much. But it seems to be the perfect bottom for wild rice to grow. The entire back channel is filled with it.

The gold and green stems shoot out of the water. There seem to be a million of them. They're typically four to six feet tall. In some spots, they're so thick we can't drive our duck boat through them.

Wild rice is the perfect side dish next to a mouthwatering duck breast drizzled with honey. And where wild rice grows is also the perfect spot for duck hunting!

The rice that falls to the bottom of the lake draws ducks from miles around. On a good fall morning, we might see a thousand ducks fill our back channel. It's a great place to rest during their long migration south. Our channel gives them some open water but also some places to hide. Most importantly, it gives them lots to eat.

We park on the beat-down grass of the front yard. Our lights shine out over our little round harbor.

Years ago, Dad and his buddies had a backhoe dig a harbor that tucks in and around the trees. This is now the perfect spot for our camo-painted flat-bottom duck boats. The harbor protects us from the angry northwest winds from the big lake.

Those winds blow all the ducks from the lake into our back channel. But oh man—when that wind is blowing, it's cold! You have to bundle up when you're out in the duck boats. Anticipating all those ducks flying right at us helps keep me warm and toasty inside too.

When Dad turns off the engine, Crystal and I jump out at the same time. The cool fall air hits me. I wish I would have thrown on my camo jacket.

But there's no time for that now. We need to get our gear into the shack and see who's here!

Chapter 2

Dad pushes open the door to the shack. The last of the white paint is trying its best to cover up the old wood.

As we file into the shack, we walk right into thick smoke coming from the cast-iron fireplace. The smoke hovers along the ceiling like a low cloud. Dad waves his hand in front of his face to create some cleaner air.

"Whew!" he says with a little cough. "Are we sending smoke signals to the neighbors?"

The gang laughs. It looks like everyone has already arrived and settled in.

"Sorry! That was me," Billy says. "I forgot to open the vent when I threw a log in."

"That's OK," Dad tells him. "At least it's warm in here!"

Billy is the same age as Crystal. His dad is Dave, my dad's friend. Billy and Dave are sitting at the green kitchen table, playing cards.

They are spitting images of each other—short and stocky. They are also quick with jokes and great shots with their shotguns. I've seen them knock down high-flying ducks like it's no problem.

Charlie and his son, Greg, are lounging in the little living room just off the kitchen. Charlie is in his favorite brown leather chair with gray duct tape covering the cracks on the armrests. This chair isn't fit for most living rooms, but it fits in perfectly at the duck shack.

Unlike Dave and Billy, Charlie and Greg are not spitting images. Charlie would fit perfectly on any pro football team's offensive line. He's big and broad. But Greg looks more like a wide receiver—tall and skinny. He has curly brown hair. He's about three years older than me.

In the corners of the room are two worn-down green fake-leather chairs. That's where Forest Crowe and Forest Lowe are sitting. They're the only guys I know named Forest, and I see them only here at the duck shack.

Forest Crowe is tall and lanky. He has thin all-white hair and a pointy, long nose. Crystal, Billy, and I have joked with one another that he looks more like a hawk, not a crow. He lives in California but comes to the duck shack every fall for two weeks. I think he is—or was—a professor. I'm not sure. All I know is that he's really smart and super interesting to talk to.

Actually, Dad has told me that both Forests are the smartest people he knows. Forest Lowe seems to win all the card games. I've heard the other dads yell and fuss about that on more than one occasion. That Forest is a regular-looking guy with graying brown hair and big glasses. His potbelly shows that he really likes good food.

We weave our way through the shack to drop off our stuff. Dad heads for the little bedroom he shares with Dave.

Crystal and I make our way to the bunk room in the back. It has four bunk beds the dads made from two-by-fours and plywood. Nothing fancy, but it gets the job done.

I dig into my duffel and pull out my favorite blue sleeping bag. I toss it up on one of the top bunks. The kids get the tops, and the adults get the bottoms. It makes sense. I can't see Forest Lowe making it to a top bunk.

Next, I open the cooler I use to store my gear. The cooler will go out with me tomorrow morning.

I count three boxes of shotgun shells. We usually don't go through that many shells in one morning, but I never want to run out. It would be horrible to watch ducks fly over that we couldn't shoot at.

I also see my favorite wooden duck call, a couple of hand warmers, some spare gloves, a Snickers bar, and my silver Thermos (perfect for hot chocolate). This is everything I need—I'm all set.

I scoot back out to the living room to join the fun. The gang is discussing where everyone plans to set up in the morning.

The two Forests say they'll do what they always do. They'll head to the back channel, find a nice opening in the wild rice, and set some decoys.

Dave and Charlie bicker back and forth about the best spot. Charlie says the Point. Dave says Nick's Pothole. Dad has told me that Dave and Charlie never agree on anything. They like to argue, just for something to do.

As the bickering continues, Greg and Billy shake their heads and laugh at their dads. They do that a lot.

All the while, my dad just sits there with a smile on his face. He wants to keep our plan quiet. We have the perfect spot picked out, and we don't want the guys from the shack racing us to it.

Then again, the other guys would have to get up pretty early to do that. We always beat everyone out the door in the morning. Dad makes sure of that.

After hanging out with the gang for about an hour more, Dad says it's time for bed. When I'm at home, I'm usually not too excited about bedtime. But when it's the night before hunting or fishing, I dive right in. It means the morning—and all the fun—is right around the corner!

I climb up to my bunk and crawl into my sleeping bag. For a few moments, I stare up at the plywood ceiling just a few feet above me. Then I close my eyes and say a quick prayer.

"Lord, thank you for this wonderful day. Thank you for all you have given me and my family. Please continue to take care of and watch over my friends and family. And . . . it sure would be great if you could send a bunch of ducks our way tomorrow. In Jesus's name, amen."

I roll over and smile about that last part. I figure it can't hurt to ask!

I close my eyes once again, settle into my pillow, and crush into sleep. Before I know it, I'll hear that magical sound . . .

Chapter 3

"Crystal, Luke—it's time to get up! Let's go!"

Dad's voice shoots through me, and my eyes pop open. Could it be morning already? Oh man, I'm still tired! No wonder— my watch says it's 5:00 a.m.

I look around the bunk room. No one else is moving. Crystal should be, but she's still asleep. Or at least pretending to be.

From my bunk, I can peek around the doorway into the kitchen. The light is on. It makes me squint. I see Dad and Charlie moving around. I'm sure they're getting their coffee going.

I take a deep breath to help myself wake up, then I carefully climb my way down the ladder. With a plop, I land on the plywood floor. After digging into my duffel, I pull on my camo pants, my wool socks, and my hoodie with a big buck on the front.

"Morning, Luke," Dad says as I make my way out to the kitchen. "Is your sister up?"

"I don't think so," I reply.

"Go get her up. We need to get going. I have your water ready for hot chocolate,"

19

he adds, nodding toward the black kettle on the stove.

Without saying a word, I turn and scoot back to the bunk room. Crystal's spot is in the far back corner. I push on her shoulder. Kinda like checking a deer after we've shot it. I'm looking for signs of life.

"Time to get up, Crystal," I say.

She doesn't budge.

I shake her harder. "Crystal! Come on. Dad's ready to go."

"*Nnnn.*" The sound barely makes it out of her mouth. "Is it morning already?"

"Yes, and Dad is ready to go. Come on."

I go back to the kitchen to make my hot chocolate. First, I empty a cocoa packet into my Thermos. Next, I need to add the hot water. It's always tricky pouring the water into the small spout, but I get it done. No way am I going out without my hot chocolate. I love the stuff.

Before long, Dad, Crystal, and I are all wearing our camo jackets, bibs, hats, and gloves. With our coolers in our hands, we head for the door.

I swivel back for one last look at the shack. Other than Charlie, nobody is really up. Yet here we are, out the door already. Just as Dad likes. Nobody can beat us to our favorite spot today!

After grabbing our shotguns from the back of the Suburban, we tromp down to the boat. We're past the reach of the yard

21

light now. The moon is out, but it's still dark. Dad pulls out his little flashlight and lights our way.

Crystal and I push our hips into the front of the boat to slide it into the water. It's calm. No wind. I watch as little ripples race from the boat across the harbor in the moonlight.

As Crystal and I steady the boat, Dad steps in and carefully makes his way to the back seat. Then Crystal climbs in. I hold up. We have to make sure the motor starts before I get in and push us off.

It takes Dad three pulls to get the motor to fire. Then it revs up with blowing smoke. The sights and sounds break through the peaceful morning.

At last, I shove the boat and roll over into my seat in the front. I do it all in one motion. I'm happy that I don't even get my boots wet. As soon as I'm settled, Dad turns the boat and points us toward the mouth of the harbor.

My eyes are slowly adjusting to the darkness. It's surprising how much I can now see. I look up and gaze upon a billion stars shining above.

That's good, because Dad needs one of those stars to guide us to our spot!

Chapter 4

"Keep your eyes on that North Star, kids," Dad says over the motor.

I look up again and scan the sky. Like magic, the Big Dipper pops out. The Big Dipper has a "handle" on one end and a "ladle" on the other. My eyes go to the top corner of the ladle, then I follow an imaginary line out into the sky.

Bam! There it is. The North Star! The biggest and brightest star off the ladle of the Big Dipper.

Dad has been teaching us this for years. The North Star is like a compass in the sky. It will always tell you which direction is north. That's good to know if you're lost or hiking in the dark.

Today, we'll follow the North Star into the back channel. Like sailors from a thousand years ago, we head right for the North Star, cutting through the water and the heavy dark.

"Where are we going?" Crystal asks.

"The Circle Bog," Dad answers.

A smile fills my face. I love the Circle Bog. We've had some amazing hunts on that baby!

A bog is a big piece of land floating on the water. You can usually walk on a bog, but you have to be careful. If you hit a hole, you can fall right through to the bottom of the lake. It's cool but also a little scary.

There are a bunch of bogs about the size of football fields scattered out in the bay. The Circle Bog is the biggest. It's just off the big open water. Ducks seem to love cruising by the Circle Bog as they head into our back channel.

After about ten minutes of chasing the North Star, Dad slows down. My eyes pierce through the darkness. I can barely make out a dark change in front of us.

Dad stands up and turns on his big Q-Beam flashlight. It's a million candle power, which is extremely bright. I'm careful not to look back when he turns it on. I made that mistake once—I was blinded for two minutes.

Dad shines the light in front of us. Suddenly, the Circle Bog appears. The golden reeds that call the bog home glow in the light.

"Never a doubt. Here we are, kids," Dad says proudly.

Dad drives the boat up onto the floating bog, which brings us to a halt. He cuts the motor. Instantly, silence fills the air.

Dad can whisper now. "We have the spot I wanted. And now we wait! In a bit, we can set out the decoys."

I lie down on my seat with my head propped on the side of the boat. I pull my knees in and point them to the sky.

There's no sign of the rising sun yet. The stars still shine like brilliant diamonds.

The sliver of a moon is tilted. It almost looks like a smile.

I take a big breath through my nose. The cool, crisp air fills my lungs. The air just seems cleaner in the dark of a new morning out on the lake.

My eyes lock onto a satellite cruising past the stars. As I follow its path, a shooting star drops like magic dust, then disappears just as quickly.

"Did you guys see that falling star?" I ask.

"Nope. I missed it," Crystal says.

Dad doesn't answer. I guess he didn't see it either.

Suddenly, I hear a motor.

"Is someone coming?" I ask.

"Sounds like it," Dad says.

The sound of a small outboard motor gets louder and louder. It's heading our way.

Dad finally turns on the Q-Beam. He shines the light toward the sound, slowly waving the beam back and forth. Then he turns it off.

It's dark again. The sound of the motor quiets.

"Shoot," we hear a voice say out in the darkness. "Someone's already there."

"Bummer," another voice says. "We'll go find another spot."

The motor starts back up, heading off in the other direction.

"And *that's* why we get up early," Dad says.

I realize now that I can see the slightest hint of light creeping over the horizon. The sun is on its way.

"Time to put out the decoys," Dad says. He starts the motor and backs us off the bog.

Crystal and I each grab a big bag of decoys. The bags are mesh, so water drains out. Each bag holds about fifteen plastic ducks.

The decoys are painted to look just like real ducks. They're mostly bluebills and a handful of mallards. Each one is connected to a thin rope about ten feet long. At the end of the rope is a lead weight the size of a golf ball.

One at a time, I unravel the rope and toss the decoy overboard. Dad directs Crystal and me where to toss them.

Our spread is something Dad takes great pride in creating. The strategy is to make two round groups of about ten decoys each. Between the groups, we leave an opening about two boat lengths wide. This gives the ducks room to land.

Then we make a long string of decoys and angle it downwind from us. For the Circle Bog, the key is having a north or northwest wind so it's blowing away from us. Ducks always land into the wind.

This special spread works like a charm. The ducks fly in, follow the angled string of decoys, then see the two round groups. That makes them want to land right in the open area we left for them.

As I send the last decoy out, Dad turns the boat back to the bog. He sweeps around the right side of the decoys and pulls the boat into a thick patch of reeds. The perfect cover.

I look up again. The stars are going to sleep now, and the horizon is filling with light.

It's time to get our guns loaded!

Chapter 5

It's time to put up our blind. The blind goes around our boat and hides and disguises us. When the ducks fly in, they won't see a boat with three people sitting in it. They'll see a small bog covered with reeds!

Dad is proud of the blind. He designed it himself. He took some plastic fencing and weaved a bunch of reeds into it. For easy setup, Dad then connected the fencing to tubes, which we slide into holes Dad screwed on to the boat.

So, all we have to do is wrap the blind around the boat and pop it into the holes. Presto! It works so well that everyone in camp uses the same design for their blinds.

Once the blind is up, we slide our shotguns out of their cases and get ready to load our shells.

I grab my box of 20-gauge shells from my cooler. First things first, I make sure my safety is on. Next, I slip a handful of shells into my right pocket for quick loading later. Then I load three of those babies into my Remington 870 pump. When I'm done, I carefully prop my gun against the blind and sit back. We are getting close to action now!

"How much time do we have before we can legally shoot?" I ask.

There are rules about when you can and cannot shoot. Dad has been teaching us this since our first hunt.

"Sunrise will be at 7:25 today, and we can shoot a half hour before sunrise. So, when does legal shooting time begin?" He poses the question back to me.

Closing my eyes for better focus, I picture a clock. I "set" the clock to 7:25, then back it up thirty minutes.

"At 6:55," I say with fairly good confidence.

"That's right. Good job."

"Lucky guess," Crystal shoots back.

Dad looks at his watch. "It's 6:40 right now, so we have only fifteen minutes to go."

Just then, I hear the hum of a motor. I look out over the blind.

"Here comes another boat." I try to see if it's anyone from our shack.

We all look out as the boat gets closer. Dad chuckles, shakes his head, and waves at the two hunters as they cruise by. We all realize it's Forest and Forest! They wave to us slowly, like they are in a parade.

"Aren't they a little late?" Crystal asks with raised eyebrows. "Shooting begins in fifteen minutes, and they're not even to their spot yet!"

Once again, Dad laughs. "As usual, those two aren't in any hurry! They feel more comfortable heading out when it's light and they can see better," Dad says.

"Not everybody likes to go out in the dark, like we do!"

We watch as their boat continues around the bog and heads into the back channel. I'm so glad we always get an early start. It's tough to wake up in the wee hours of the morning. But we always get the spot we want, and it gives us plenty of time to settle in and get ready.

And now there are less than fifteen minutes to go. I'm pumped! I can't wait for that first duck!

As if on cue, I hear the sound of wings whistling above. A huge flock of ducks races over our heads like a black cloud.

"Oh man! That would be a great shot! It's close enough to legal shooting time, isn't it, Dad?" I plea.

"'Close enough' doesn't count," he says, shaking his head firmly. "You know we always follow the rules. Shooting time begins at 6:55. And we will not be shooting a second early."

Suddenly, *BOOM! BOOM!* thunders across the lake. Someone else is shooting!

"See? They are shooting already," I argue to Dad.

He shakes his head slowly, unconvinced. "That doesn't make it right. Rules are rules, and we each must decide if we're going to follow them. Those people can make their own decisions. We will make ours."

I let out a sigh. "You're right, Dad. We can wait a few minutes. It's the right thing to do."

More ducks fly over. The anticipation is killing me!

Then, out of nowhere, two ducks skid to a landing right by our decoys. They start quacking. They're clearly mallards. I can tell by their loud quacks and their shape.

"That's cool," Crystal whispers. "They have no idea we're here."

"Remember, though," Dad says, "we don't shoot ducks on the water."

"Why? Is that illegal too?" I ask, forgetting the details.

"No. You can legally shoot ducks sitting on the water," Dad explains. "But it just doesn't seem right to me. A lot of other hunters feel the same way. Ever heard of something or someone called a 'sitting duck'?"

"Yeah," I say. "That means you're a really easy target!"

"Exactly," Dad says. "It doesn't feel right to take such an easy shot. Hunting is a *sport*. And good sportsmanship means there should be a sense of fair play. At least when ducks are flying, they have a fair chance against us. We don't hit them all!"

I nod. It makes sense.

"So, flying ducks only, it is." I am excited for the challenge.

"This seems like a good time for our quick safety talk." Dad is always teaching us. "What's rule number one?"

"Keep your trigger safety on at all times, unless we are shooting," Crystal and I say in perfect unison.

"Rule number two?" Dad asks.

"Always keep your gun barrel pointing up until you are ready to shoot." Crystal makes a check mark in the air with her finger.

"And rule number three?"

"Never shoot over anyone's head," I say quickly, beating Crystal to it by a second.

"And rule number four?"

"Have fun!" we both say.

"Following that rule won't be a problem!" I add.

"You guys have this all figured out! Good job!" Dad says.

He smiles as he puts a hand on Crystal's shoulder and looks back and forth between her and me.

"And by the way, thanks for hunting with me. I love having you both here!"

"Well, we are pretty lucky that you bring us. Thank you," Crystal says, smiling back.

"By the way, is it time yet? Is it 6:55?" I whisper with hope.

"One more minute," Dad says, checking his watch for a second time.

One minute! I pick up my 20-gauge, check the safety, then hold my gun tight to my chest. I love this gun. The stock is the perfect length. It fits right to my cheek when I pull it up to shoot. Also, it's not too heavy. It just feels good when I swing on a bird.

I close my eyes and wait to hear the magic words . . .

"Game on, guys! It's legal shooting time!" Dad whispers with excitement.

My eyes pop open, and a big smile fills my face.

"Bring 'em on!"

Chapter 6

My pointer finger rubs the top of my safety. I can feel it just fine through my light glove. At a moment's notice, I can unlock it and be ready to shoot. It's go time!

Usually, we get our best chances for shooting in the first half hour. But it can be tricky too. Sometimes the ducks appear out of nowhere and surprise you.

I scan the horizon, looking for any dark spot that might be a duck. Suddenly, I hear wings whistling. I quickly look up and freeze, trying to locate the flying ducks.

"Straight up. But way too high," Crystal says.

I can see them now too. It's a flock of about ten ducks, racing through the sky.

"West!" Dad whispers loudly, pulling my attention away.

Which way is west? I think to myself.

I quickly picture a compass in my head and think of the trick Grandpa taught me. The *W* for west is on the left side of the compass. The *E* for east is on the right. Left to right, you can read it like the word *WE*. And I know north is behind us, because we followed the North Star to the bog. So, I imagine turning around to face north, then

I picture the word *WE*. That means west is my side of the boat!

I look to my right, and yep—two ducks are flying ten feet off the water. They're coming toward our decoys. I ready my gun.

"Take 'em!" Dad says.

I straighten up, push off my safety, and find the lead bird as I look down my barrel. It's just like throwing a football to a receiver on the move. You have to throw the pass just a little in front of them. So I aim a little in front of the duck, and when it feels right, I quickly squeeze the trigger.

BOOM!

The duck folds up and crashes to the water, in the middle of our decoys.

BOOM!

That one is Crystal. The second duck drops.

"Oh yeah! Nice shooting, kids!" Dad calls out.

Crystal looks at me with a big smile. "And that's how it's done!"

We push our safeties back on and then fist-bump with flare.

I set my trusty 20-gauge against my seat. You can't picture a bigger smile than the one I'm wearing right now. There's no greater challenge than hitting a fast-flying duck. Especially the first one of the year.

"Let's go pick those up and get them in the boat," Dad says.

Dad brings the motor to life and jams it into reverse. We need to free ourselves from the bog, so Dad revs up the engine. Crystal and I rock back and forth to help move the boat. Finally, we're free.

Dad cruises over to the ducks, being careful not to snag a decoy line with the motor. Then I snatch up each duck with a fishing net we've spray-painted brown. Without the net, it's hard to reach over the blind material wrapped around the boat.

Up close, we can see they are two perfect green-head mallards. Legally, we can take fifteen ducks between the three of us.

Two down. Thirteen to go.

Dad races us back so we can slide into the same spot as before.

"Keep 'em coming," Dad says.

Grabbing my gun, I check the safety. Then I pull a shell out of my pocket and slide it in my gun. Back to three and fully loaded! With laser-focused eyes, I search the sky, looking for another flying duck.

Then Dad suddenly comes to life and startles me.

"Duck!" he yells.

Crystal and I don't even have time to react. All we can do is watch as Dad jumps up and lets a shot fly. A lone green-winged teal races by. Green-winged teals are the smallest duck in our area. This one is zooming just above the water. It zips between our decoys at what seems to be one hundred miles per hour.

"Whoa, he was going fast," Dad says, settling back down.

I go back to scanning the horizon. I can see a nice flock circling far out in front of us. I keep my eyes on them as they zig and zag over the water. If they notice our decoy line, maybe they'll come toward us.

Sure enough, they turn. Now they're heading right our way.

"South! Coming right in," I say, getting the hang of this direction stuff.

"I see 'em," Crystal says.

"That's a good-looking group," Dad adds.

"Get ready!" Dad's as excited as we are.

All three of us lock in on them. I've got my gun up and my finger on the safety. They're coming right in—like a swarm of bees chasing a bear who just knocked down their hive. And then the lead ducks dive for the gap we left for them in between our two groups of decoys. The rest are hot on their heels.

"Take 'em!" Dad barks.

I push off my safety and lock on the duck closest to me. I pull in front of it and shoot.

The duck flares straight up, due to either the sound of our shots or the feeling of a bunch of BBs flying by it. Maybe both.

I missed!

I pump another shell into the chamber and lock on the same duck. I shoot again.

Nothing!

I pump my last shell in. I let one more shot go just as the duck turns.

It doesn't flinch. It joins the rest of the flock as they race away to safety.

I'm oh for three.

"Darn it!" I mutter.

When I look over, Dad and Crystal are high-fiving. Dad knocked down two, which we call a double. Crystal got one.

"Did you get one, Luke?" Crystal asks.

With tight lips and a steady shake of my head, I must admit defeat. "Nope. I missed. I can't believe it, but I did.

We race out and pick up the three ducks. They're all ringbills, which are divers. That means they dive to the bottom of lakes to get their food. The cool thing about divers is that they usually fly in big flocks. When they come in, it's super cool. Later in the fall, it's common to see flocks with as many as fifty to one hundred ringbills.

"Good shooting! That makes five ducks in the boat," Dad says.

"Yeah, and we would've had one or two more if Luke had helped us out there," Crystal teases.

"Yeah, yeah." I laugh a little with her. "I'll get 'em next time."

"You bet you will, Luke," Dad says with a smile full of confidence.

Duck hunting is like any other sport. You can't give up. Sometimes baseball players strike out. Sometimes quarterbacks throw incomplete passes. That doesn't mean they quit. Missing is part of the game.

I can't wait for another chance. I'm on full alert now!

Chapter 7

Five mallards pass over us, out in front of the decoys. They don't seem interested in our setup, though. They're flying right on by.

"Give them a call, Luke," Dad says.

When you call ducks, you use a special call made out of plastic or wood to make realistic quacking noises to get the ducks' attention. It's like talking to ducks in their own language. You can't just make a bunch of random quacks and expect it to work. There are specific calls for specific moments. I've been practicing, because that's the key to learning any language.

Quickly opening my cooler, I grab my duck call. I take a deep breath and let out a call as loud as I can blow. This one is called a hail call.

Quaaaack, quack-quack, quack, quack, quack . . . !

In duck language, that's how a duck on the water would beg for a flying flock to turn around and come back. And sure enough—I can't believe my eyes when the whole flock takes a hard-left turn and heads straight at us.

"You turned them, Luke!" Dad's smile is big and proud. "Good job!"

I smile and nod. I'm super pumped that all my practice paid off!

I give a few softer quacks as the flock commits to coming in. Then I set my call down and grab my gun. We're crouched down, like lions hiding in the grass, ready to pounce!

All at once, the five mallards cup their wings and zigzag right into our decoys.

"Take 'em!" Dad says.

I pull up my gun and see a giant green head flare my way. The end of my barrel is like a heat-seeking missile. I stick with him. I aim just out in front of his beak, then let the shot fly. He folds up and crashes to the water.

"Yes!"

Several other shots boom. Two more ducks fall from the sky. They splash, one after the other.

"Oh yeah! Nice shooting, kids," Dad says. "Three green heads on the water."

"That was sweet! Did you get one, Crystal?" I ask.

"Yep. Took me three shots, but I got him."

Again, we race out and scoop up the ducks. On the way back to the bog, I hold my beautiful drake mallard in my hands and check out his feathers.

He has the greenest head and two big curls on his tail. The more curls, the bigger and older the duck. That's what Dad taught us.

Oh, this guy is gonna taste good when we cook him up!

I set him with the others on the bottom of the boat, and we pull back into our spot. It's easier to slide in now. The bog is getting beat down.

"That makes eight," Crystal says.

"Our limit is five ducks apiece this year, right, Dad?" I ask.

"That's correct."

The words don't get out of his mouth before Crystal grabs her gun. I can tell by the look in her eyes that something is coming. By the time I look up, two ducks are right over our decoys. I'm too late—no chance for me. Dad and I look on as Crystal jumps up and launches two shots.

Clean misses!

Crystal slaps her right leg in disgust. "Shoot! I thought I was on them!"

"What a time to miss—right when we're watching!" I joke.

"It happens to the best of us," Dad adds, trying to boost her confidence. "You'll get the next one."

Luckily, we don't have time to worry about those missed ducks. Two more ducks are circling out front. They see our decoys and are streaming right toward us.

We don't have to say a word. All three of us are locked on them.

But then at the last second, the ducks must see something they don't like. Instead of coming in, they flare up and away on Dad's side.

Dad leaps up and takes one shot. That's all he has time for.

The two ducks don't flinch. They keep racing away.

When Dad turns around, his face is serious. "I decided to be nice and let them go."

Crystal cocks her head and gives Dad "the look." She and I both know well and good that he didn't just "let them go."

After a few seconds, we all break out laughing.

"See?" Dad says, sitting back down. "Even I miss once in a while!"

My eyes go back to scanning. Like an eagle looking for dinner, I focus hard. The trick is to move your eyes slowly back and forth while keeping your head still. That makes it easier to catch the movement of a flying duck.

I'm watching to the west, Crystal to the south, and Dad to the east. We're a team—us against the ducks. Still, I take great pride in being the first to see incoming ducks. Spotting them first means I'm doing my job and paying attention!

By this point in the morning, the sun has finally reached out above the trees in the eastern sky. Quite a difference compared to the moonlight we started out in.

While the sunlight is nice, it's also a little tricky. It makes it hard to watch the sky. We're thankful when some clouds blow in and block the sun. No one is more thankful than Dad. With him watching the east, the sun has been hitting him right in the eyes.

Along with the clouds rolling in, a northwest wind picks up too. That's sure to help. That will push ducks into our bay. It'll also make the decoys look more lifelike as they move in the breeze.

I gaze out at the decoys, watching them bob and sway. It's a little hypnotizing. But that lasts only a second.

"Southeast!" Dad suddenly says. "Here they come. Get ready, kids!"

Chapter 8

Picturing a compass once again, I know just where to look. Scanning the southeast horizon, I see them. A nice flock of divers.

"Got 'em!" I say.

"Me too," adds Crystal.

The flock moves as one. They all turn left, then right. With each movement, they never come out of form. Then they turn and follow our decoy line, right to us. It's like pulling them in with a magnet.

My heart pounds with excitement. My finger is alert, ready to push my safety at any second.

"Take 'em!" Dad says.

We jump up. But as soon as we do, the ducks flare and split into two groups. There's a group on each side of the decoy spread.

I chase the lead bird on my side. I want to make this first shot count—and I do. I drop him!

I pump in another round and chase the second bird with my barrel. I pull in front of him and shoot.

That one I miss.

I pump in my last round and take one more blast at him.

Bummer! I miss again!

I'm frustrated that I missed my last two shots, but I'm excited that I dropped the first bird. That's duck hunting. Just when you think you've got it all figured out, you miss, and it sets you in your place. It's hard to hit a flying duck.

But it's super fun trying!

"How many do we have down?" Dad asks. "I dropped one."

"I got one," Crystal adds.

"Me too—one down."

"Let's go pick them up." Dad starts the motor with one pull.

We're off, then back in a flash. We now have eleven of our fifteen ducks. This has been an awesome morning!

Then I hear a grumbling sound. It's my stomach calling for some food! We haven't eaten anything yet today.

"Hey, Dad—could I have a doughnut?" I ask.

"You bet. This seems like a perfect time for a break."

Dad digs into his cooler and pulls out the box of old-fashioned doughnuts. My mouth starts watering as I think about that first bite. I grab one and set it down on the seat. (A little dirt never hurt me.)

I reach into my cooler, grab my Thermos, and unscrew the cap. Steam rises out like a python snake. The cap doubles as a cup. I fill it to the top with my creamy hot chocolate.

Finally ready now, I break my doughnut in half and dip it into my hot chocolate. The dripping, hot bite melts in my mouth.

"Oh baby. That's good!" I say. "Crystal, you have to try dipping it in your hot chocolate!"

She gives it a try. The look on her face says it all. She knows I'm onto something good.

Looking over, I see Dad dip his doughnut into his coffee. He takes a bite, smiles, and nods at me. I guess that means it works with coffee too. Not that you're gonna catch *me* trying it!

All of a sudden, Dad bolts up straight in his seat. "Ducks!" he says through a mouthful of doughnut. He rushes to put his coffee down and grab for his gun.

I sneak one more bite before I set my doughnut and hot chocolate down. Chewing, I grab my gun and look out.

A small flock is bombing in. How dare they interrupt our break?

Swallowing the doughnut, I jump up and pull my gun to my cheek. I chase one of the ducks, getting ready to shoot.

But before I can pull the trigger, the duck drops from my sight. At the same moment, Crystal lets out a cheer. She nailed it before I even had the chance!

I move to another duck. But once again, it falls from the sky just before I'm about to shoot. Dad got that one.

Before I can try for a third time, the other ducks escape. It's over. And Dad and Crystal are high-fiving again.

"Nice shooting, you two," I say with a little laugh. "It didn't work out so great for me, though. You were each a second ahead of me."

"Sorry, Luke!" Dad says. He raises his shoulders toward his ears and holds out his hands. "We didn't *mean* to."

Now we're all laughing.

We head out to gather the ducks, then we return to our spot on the bog.

"At least we can get back to our doughnuts," I say.

I drop to my seat and start dunking again. With a contented smile, I chase my drenched doughnut down with a sip of hot chocolate.

What a morning! Perfect weather. Lots of ducks. And our favorite doughnuts to boot. This is yet another amazing opener.

Just as I swallow the last bite of my hot-chocolate-dipped doughnut, I hear a sound. All three of us freeze and focus.

Honking!

But this honk isn't from a car.

My eyes pop wide open, and I look at Crystal and Dad.

"Geese!"

Chapter 9

What a shock—geese! Duck season and goose season both start today. Lucky for us, our licenses are good for either one. However, we don't usually see many geese on the duck opener. This is a huge bonus!

Crystal scrambles for her cooler. She digs in and pulls out her goose call. Forest Crowe gave it to her last year. He said he wasn't any good at sounding like a goose. He thought maybe Crystal could figure it out. And she did.

She practiced a bunch last summer. Crystal sounded so real that one neighbor assumed we had a pet goose. She came over and asked us if we could keep it quiet. After she left, Crystal and I laughed until tears were flowing.

I look up at the sky as the honking gets louder. Now we can see a nice-sized flock of geese out over the big water. There are probably ten or twelve in the group. They're fairly low and kind of heading our way.

"Let's see what you can do, Crystal," I say with hope, nodding to the call in her hands.

She starts with a few honks. *Honk, honk.* Then she blows harder and harder. *HONK! HONK! HONK!* In goose language, it sounds like a goose really wants company!

To our surprise, the flock begins honking louder. They make a slow left turn toward us.

"It's working! You got them to turn," Dad says, getting fired up.

"Come on, Crystal—you can do this. Bring them in!" I can't wait to get a shot at a goose.

She goes loud, then soft, and then she adds some long runs of honks. *HONK! Honk. Honk-honk-honk-honk.* She really sounds like a goose!

The flock is even lower now and still heading right to us. My heart pounds. I've never shot a goose before. But this is happening!

"Ease up now—let them come in," Dad whispers, coaching Crystal.

The geese are halfway down our decoy line. I'm amazed they're following our *duck* line. How cool is that?

One or two of them honk, here and there. It's like they're talking to one another, confirming their landing spot. The closer they get, the bigger they are. It's like I'm watching a movie. I can't believe my eyes.

Now their wings are set and cupped, which helps slow them down. They glide in like 747 airplanes. They are *huge*! My eyes grow bigger and bigger the closer they get. I hold my breath. I don't want anything to mess this up.

Then I hear the magic words.

"Take 'em!"

We jump up and let the shots fly. I pick the goose closest to me. I put my bead right on his head and pull the trigger.

He flares straight up. I missed!

In a flash, I pump in another shell. This time, I pull the barrel just above his head—not right on it. As I pull the trigger, I keep moving my barrel in front of him.

It works! The giant Canadian honker folds up and seems to freeze in midair. Then gravity takes over, and he falls from the sky like a giant boulder.

Looking down my barrel, I follow him all the way to the water. He makes a huge splash. He doesn't move an inch, but I'm ready with another shot, if needed. There's no way this goose is getting away!

When it's all over, three giant honkers float in the water.

"*Oh yeah!*" I howl. "That was amazing! My first goose!" I cannot contain myself.

"I got one too!" Crystal smiles from ear to ear.

"That makes all three of us," Dad says. "Good shooting, team!"

"Way to call those babies in, Crystal," I add. "You were amazing!"

"Thanks, buddy. My guiding services are always available," she replies with a wink.

We hurry out to pick up our prizes. I quickly realize we have a challenge on our hands. The geese are way too big for the little fishing net we use to scoop up ducks. Instead, Dad has to maneuver the boat right up to them. Then he reaches down with his hand and lugs the geese over the back of the boat.

Once we get them in, I can see up close just how giant and cool they are. I hold up the one I got. When I open his wings, they stretch as wide and far as my arms stretch.

"Looks like there will be a change of plans for Thanksgiving dinner," Dad says, smiling. "Forget turkey—there will be smoked goose on the menu."

"That sounds awesome," Crystal says. "I can't wait!"

"All we need now is two more ducks, and then we can head in for breakfast," Dad says.

Even though we're having so much fun out here, I have to admit I'm getting hungry. Dad's famous scrambled eggs with maple sausage do sound rather good right now.

If we need two more ducks, then we better speed things up—and I know just how to do it.

I pull out my trusty duck call and sound off a few hails. As if by magic, a flock of mallards appears, circling around the bog. I call a few more times.

"Get ready, kids," Dad says. "They're coming in!"

Chapter 10

"Way to call them, Luke!" Crystal says. "Me with the goose call, and you with the duck call!"

"Looks like you two are earning your keep on this hunt," Dad jokes.

For the fun of it, I make a few light calls to keep the mallards coming. And they do. Maybe it's because of my calling. Or maybe it's because of our decoys. It doesn't really matter. Either way, the ducks are coming!

"Get ready—this could be good," Dad whispers, keeping his head below the blind. After a second, he quietly calls out, "Take 'em!"

We rise up right at the perfect time. We totally surprise them.

I quickly pick out a big green head and chase him with my barrel. Once I pull in front of him, I let the shot fly.

He instantly folds up and drops to the water.

Without wasting time, I pump in another shell and track down another green head. Once again, I quickly pull in front and take the shot.

I can hardly believe it when he folds and crashes to the water too.

A double! My first double! I shot two ducks from the same flock!

"Yeah, baby!" I shout.

"Way to go, Lucky Luke! Good job!" Dad gives me a thumbs-up.

"Sweet shooting, buddy!" Crystal says, sending me a fist bump.

After the smoke settles, we have two mallards in the water.

"And that makes a limit!" Dad says. "Good shooting. What an amazing opener."

Just then, two wood ducks turn and come right for us.

"Two more are coming!" I crouch down and ready my gun.

Dad looks over at me and shakes his head. "We're done—we have our limit."

"But they're coming right at us," I plead. "We can't pass on them! Come on—one more chance!"

Dad stands up and shakes his head firmly this time. "Nope. Unload your guns, kids. We have our limit. We are done. That's the rule."

The two ducks fly right over our heads. All I can do is watch them disappear.

I love hunting so much. It's hard to stop. But Dad is right. Rules are rules.

As I unload my gun, I think about the shots we heard before legal shooting time began this morning. As Dad said, we all have to make our choices. And live with the consequences. I'm glad we're making the decision to not go over the limit. Now I remember Grandpa telling me once, "If you follow the rules, you don't have to worry about getting caught." That makes more sense now.

We take down the blind, then Dad steps out onto a firm spot of the bog. "Hold up some ducks, kids. I want a picture to remember this special day."

Crystal and I each grab one of the giant mallards we shot. Dad snaps a couple of pictures and then steps back into the boat.

It takes us about a half hour to pick up all our decoys. The hard work and cold, wet hands are worth every minute, though. I'm excited to head back to the shack and see if anyone else limited out. I'm also excited for breakfast, because I'm starving!

I sit next to Crystal in the middle seat as we race back to the shack. I gaze at the pile of ducks and geese on the bottom of the boat, and I can't help but smile.

Duck hunting is amazing. We are so lucky Dad takes us out. What an adventure! What a morning!

And tomorrow, we get to do it again!

About the Author

Kevin Lovegreen was born, raised, and lives in Minnesota with his loving wife and two amazing children. Hunting, fishing, and the outdoors have always been a big part of his life. From chasing squirrels as a child to chasing elk as an adult, Kevin loves the thrill of hunting. But even more, he loves telling the stories of the adventure. Presenting at schools and connecting with kids about the outdoors is one of his favorite things to do.

Monster Mule Deer

Lucky Luke's
25lb. turkey

The
Muddy
Elk

Crystal's
1st buck

Lucky Luke
with a large-
mouth bass

Lucky Luke's
1st bear

Crystal, The Swamp hero!

www.KevinLovegreen.com

Other books in the series

To order books or learn about
school visits please go to:
www.KevinLovegreen.com

All the stories in the Lucky Luke's Hunting Adventures series are based on real experiences that happened to me or my family.

If you like the book, please help spread the word by telling all your friends!

Thanks for reading!
Kevin Lovegreen